REBEL GIRLS

Little Library

10 Women who Love Science

Good Night Stories for Rebel Girls and all other Rebel Girls titles are available for bulk purchase for sale promotions, premiums, fundraising, and educational needs. For details, write to sales@rebelgirls.com.

www.rebelgirls.com

Rebel Girls, Inc.
421 Elm Ave.
Larkspur, CA 94939

Text by Dinah Dunn
Art direction by Giulia Flamini
Graphic design by Kristen Brittain
Graphic design and additional illustrations: Alessandro Raimondo
Portrait illustrations: 4: Janice Chang, 8: Iliana Galvez,
12: Martina Paukova, 16: Keturah Ariel, 20: Claudia Carieri,
24: Gaby Verdooren, 28: Martina Paukova, 32: Sarah Wilkins,
36: Eva Rust, 40: Aurelia Durand.

Printed in China, 2023
10 9 8 7 6 5 4 3 2 1
ISBN: 979-8-88964-079-0

FSC
www.fsc.org
MIX
Paper | Supporting responsible forestry
FSC™ C018179

CONTENTS

Amber Yang

Computer Scientist and Entrepreneur

Born circa 1999 | USA

Most kids want to go to Disney World. Not Amber! She wanted to go to the Kennedy Space Center. There, rockets blasted off to space. There was also a museum. Amber learned about stars, planets, and spaceships.

In preschool, a group of boys were playing with a toy spaceship. Amber wanted to pretend to be an astronaut with them. The boys said she couldn't because she was a girl. It was not the last time Amber was told she couldn't do something. She joined a robotics team in middle school. A boy said, *Do you even know how to do anything? You can just sit and watch.*

Amber knew they were wrong. She wanted to prove how much she knew about science. In high school, she watched a film about astronauts. In it, space debris destroyed a spacecraft. Space debris is any object that humans leave up in space. It scared her. She decided to learn more.

She learned there were already a million pieces of space debris around Earth. Some traveled as fast as 17,500 miles per hour—30 times as fast as an airplane! Each time a piece of debris bumps into another, it breaks apart and makes more. All that debris can damage spaceships. Something needed to be done!

So Amber set out to find a way to keep spacecraft safe. She did months of research. She created a computer program that finds space debris. That way spacecraft can move out of its way. She turned her project into a company called Seer Tracking.

Amber hopes her program will also inspire people to clean up space. "My biggest dream is being a part of the conversation of what space will look like," she says. Amber is not sitting and watching—she is making change happen!

Darcie Little Badger

Earth Scientist and Writer

Born 1987 | USA and Lipan Apache

Darcie was studying earth science in college. She went on a research trip to Bermuda. There, she rode a tiny boat far out in the ocean. As she floated in the cool blue water, she wondered what lay in the deep below her.

Darcie hadn't realized how amazing the ocean could be. There were creatures down there that no one could even imagine! She went back to her home state of Texas to learn about oceanography.

Darcie had always enjoyed imagining different worlds. She loved the stories her mom and her grandma Elatsoe told her when she was growing up. The tales came from their Lipan Apache tribe. They had ghosts, monsters, and animals. Sometimes, they were scary.

Darcie wanted to find more stories about Lipan Apache people. She went to libraries and bookstores. She couldn't find a single book! So in first grade, she decided to write one herself. Her father helped her send it to a couple of publishers. That first book wasn't published. But Darcie still kept writing.

When she got older, she combined her two loves: writing and science. Her first book for young adults is called *Elatsoe*, after her grandmother. That and her second book, *A Snake Falls to Earth*, have Lipan Apache

characters. People love both books, which have won a lot of awards.

Darcie uses what she knows about science to write science fiction. Her books feature animal spirits who live with the human characters. And *A Snake Falls to Earth* is set in Texas in the future. In it, she imagines what climate change could to do the area.

Darcie feels proud to write books with Lipan Apache characters. At first, she wasn't sure if anyone would read them. But, she said, "I wrote them anyway because they're the stories of my heart."

Katia Krafft

Volcanologist

April 17, 1942–June 3, 1991 | France

Katia loved volcanoes. But she didn't just like to look at pictures of rivers of hot lava. She wanted to see them for real.

In college, Katia met a young man named Maurice who felt the same way about volcanoes. On their first date, they realized they shared a dream. They both wanted to film a volcano as it was erupting. No one had ever done that before.

Katia and Maurice fell in love. They planned their first trip to an active volcano. It was as beautiful as they had imagined.

From then on, they were hooked. "Once you see an eruption, you can't live without it," said Katia. Whenever they heard that a volcano was about

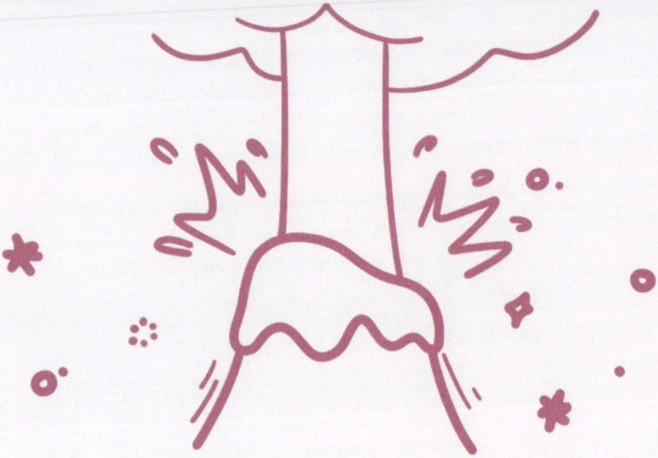

to blow, they packed their bags and rushed there.

To get the best shots, they would climb up to the edge of the crater. They wore silver suits and helmets so they wouldn't burn. The lava was more than 1,000 degrees!

Few scientists studied volcanoes up close. Katia and Maurice's research helped people stay safe from eruptions. But their work could be very dangerous.

One day in 1991, Katia and Maurice were on Mount Unzen, an active volcano in Japan. They thought they were a safe distance from the top. But they were wrong.

The explosion was larger than anyone expected. It sent a cloud of gases, rocks, and ash rolling down the valley. Katia and Maurice could not escape. They died in the blast.

People still remember Katia's work today. She inspired other women to be brave enough to study volcanoes.

SCAN TO HEAR MORE!

Environmentalist

Born December 7, 1989 | The Bahamas

Once there lived a girl in the Bahamas who swam in the sea every day. Kristal loved the way the cool water felt against her skin. She loved laughing and playing in the sand with her family. At a young age, Kristal knew she wanted to become a scientist who studied the ocean.

Working at an aquarium as a teenager changed her life. One day, Kristal had to help a sea turtle that had swallowed plastic. It broke her heart to see an animal in pain because of pollution in the ocean.

Kristal made a promise. She would never drop plastic on the ground again. And she would do all she could to keep the oceans clean and sea creatures safe.

But everywhere she looked, she saw water bottles, jugs, and torn plastic bags. Litter covered the beaches. *These beaches should be filled with tiny crabs, birds, and playing children*, Kristal thought.

Kristal got more involved in making that happen. She started the Bahamas Plastic Movement to help get rid of plastic waste. She also started a free summer camp. There, kids learned about how to help protect animals in the ocean.

Kristal and her students wrote a bill that would stop some plastic from being used in the Bahamas. They met with people in the government. Together, they raised their voices and sang, "We are the change. We are the solution. We can fix this plastic pollution!"

In 2018, the bill passed! One ocean-loving young woman lifted her voice and protected the shores she loved so much. When Kristal won a prize for her work, she said, "It is not just a win for me, but a win for the Bahamas." It was also a win for Black women in the sciences.

Marie Curie

Scientist

November 7, 1867–July 4, 1934 | Poland and France

Marie was always hungry to learn. Luckily, Marie's father was a teacher. Women weren't allowed to become scientists in Poland at the time. After she got out of high school, he taught her physics and math at home. But she didn't have a lab, so she couldn't do experiments.

One day, Marie's sister asked if she wanted to live with her in Paris. Marie could go to a school called the Sorbonne. Finally, she could go to college!

When she got in, Marie didn't know as much as the other students. She worked hard to catch up.

Marie was interested in metals and magnets. She found out that some minerals were radioactive. That meant they gave off powerful rays and glowed in the dark.

To study them, Marie would set them on fire, melt them, and stay up all night to watch them glow. She was not afraid to try new things.

Marie's husband, Pierre, was also a scientist. Together, they discovered two new radioactive elements: polonium and radium.

Radiation is now used to treat many diseases. But it is also very dangerous. If you want to be close to it, you have to wear special clothing and gloves. Both Marie and Pierre sometimes got sick working with it.

They won a Nobel Prize for their discoveries. Marie won a second Nobel Prize after Pierre's death. The Sorbonne even built Marie her own laboratory! There, she studied and made new inventions.

One thing she invented was an X-ray machine. She and her daughter helped doctors use it on soldiers injured during World War I. Marie could have made a lot of money from her discoveries. But she gave them away for free. She wouldn't let money get in the way of someone else's learning.

SCAN TO HEAR MORE!

Maritza Soto Vásquez

Astronomer

Born 1990 | Chile

Once upon a time in Chile, a child named Maritza fell in love with the night sky. While other kids played outside, Maritza curled up in a chair and read her parents' encyclopedias. Before computers, these big, heavy books could tell her anything she wanted to know. It was like the whole world opened up to her in those pages! She learned about everything she could.

Space was the subject she liked best. She read many books, looking at the photos of planets, stars, and meteor showers. Later, she would look at the twinkling up in the night sky. Maritza imagined what it would be like to find a planet no one had ever seen before.

One day, Maritza got her chance. For months in college, she'd been studying a solar system. It seemed a lot like ours, with planets and a star. But then she noticed something new. She saw an object moving around the star in a circle. That was just like the way Earth goes around the Sun.

What could that be? Maritza wondered. Looking through her telescope, she realized what she was seeing. She'd discovered a planet bigger than Earth! It was even bigger than Jupiter. Imagine filling a bowl with 4,000 Earths—that's how big this planet was!

Maritza was very proud. After years of reading about other astronomers' discoveries, Maritza had found a planet of her very own. A few years later, she discovered two more. Who knows how many more she will find!

Paleontologist

May 21, 1799–March 9, 1847 | UK

In a tiny house on the southern coast of England, there lived a girl called Mary. The winds and storms often beat up the coast. After they passed, fossils could be seen in the cliffs along the shore. Fossils are what is left of plants or animals that died a long time ago.

Mary's family was too poor to pay for her to go to school. But she still learned to read and write. And she went with her dad to find fossils. She taught herself about rocks. She also learned about the skeletons of animals. That way she could understand the fossils she found in the cliffs.

One day when she was 12, Mary's dad found a weird skull. She took

out her special
little hammer.
Tap, tap, tap!
She started
chipping away
at the rock around
the skull. Over seven
months, she uncovered a 30-foot-long skeleton. It had a long beak, but it wasn't a bird. It had rows of sharp teeth, but it wasn't a shark. It had flippers, but it wasn't a fish. It even had a long, thin tail!

Mary had made the first ever discovery of that kind of fossil. She named it *ichthyosaur*, meaning "fish-lizard." When she got older, she also uncovered the complete skeleton of what she called a *plesiosaurus*, which was an ancient reptile that lived in the sea. These were just two of her many discoveries.

At the time, people believed that the Earth was only a few thousand years old. Mary's fossils showed that was wrong. There had been life on our planet for hundreds of millions of years. Scientists from all over the world came to see the creatures Mary uncovered.

Rachel Carson

Environmentalist

May 27, 1907–April 14, 1964 | USA

Once there was a girl who loved to write stories about animals. Her name was Rachel. She grew up in the country, where her mom taught her to love nature. She was so good at writing that she published her first story at 10 years old.

Rachel studied animals in college. When she graduated, she found a job writing a series of radio shows about fish. Somehow, she made that topic exciting! Rachel's program, called *Romance Under the Waters*, was a big hit.

Soon, Rachel was in charge of all books and articles for the US Fish and Wildlife Services, a part of the government that protects animals. She was busy, but she also cared for

her two nieces after her sister died. And she still found time to write two beautiful books. *The Sea Around Us* and *The Edge of the Sea* were both bestsellers.

Years later, Rachel learned about something that made her worried. Farmers were using chemicals on crops to stop bugs from eating them. It worked, but now many birds were dying. Rachel discovered that these chemicals were poisoning other plants, animals, birds, and even humans. What could Rachel do?

She wrote a book about it called *Silent Spring*. She wanted people to see the beauty of nature and what chemicals could do to it. She wrote, "One way to open your eyes to unnoticed beauty is to ask yourself, 'What if I had never seen this before? What if I knew I would never see it again?'"

The people who sold these chemicals tried to stop her. But Rachel kept telling people what she'd learned. *Silent Spring* was voted one of the most important science books ever written. It has helped millions of people care about the environment. It also made people understand how all creatures are connected.

SCAN TO HEAR MORE!

Sara Mazrouei

Planetary Scientist

Born November 3, 1987 | Iran and Canada

Once there was a girl in Iran who wanted a life as exciting as seeing a comet in the night sky. Sara loved reading books about space and brave girls who weren't afraid to be different.

Iran didn't allow women to learn the same things as men. Her parents wanted Sara and her sisters to be able to study and become whatever they wanted. So when Sara was 13, her family moved to Canada.

Sara dreamed of being a scientist at NASA, a space program in the United States. While she was in college, she was chosen to work with other students at NASA.

A few weeks after she arrived, Sara got terrible news. She couldn't visit the Johnson Space Center with the other students.

The American government said she was too much of a risk. She had been born in Iran, an enemy of the United States. *How did you get this job in the first place?* they asked.

Sara was upset. She had never hidden where she was born. But she finished the job, got her degree, and became a planetary scientist. She went on to teach others about space. She studied asteroids. She helped figure out the best landing spots for future trips to the moon.

Sara always had to defend her right to do her job. Sometimes she wondered how much more she could have done if she didn't have to fight all the time. She stands up for everyone's right to have the career they want. Being a woman or being from Iran shouldn't stop them. Just like it didn't stop her.

Timnit Gebru

Computer Scientist

Birthdate Unknown | Ethiopia and USA

Timnit's house in Ethiopia was filled with people who loved numbers and science. When you had a problem, you found a way to fix it. Timnit would continue to do that for the rest of her life.

When Timnit was a teenager, war broke out between Ethiopia and Eritrea. Timnit's family had come from Eritrea, so they had to leave Ethiopia. They moved to the United States. It was safer for them there.

When Timnit started high school in Massachusetts, she asked to be put in the hardest math and science classes. Her teachers didn't think it was a good idea. *A student from Africa can't do this work*, some said. Timnit decided to prove them wrong.

She finished high school, got into Stanford University, and studied electrical engineering. In graduate school, she also started working on computers at Apple. There, Timnit became interested in teaching computers to learn like humans. That is called artificial intelligence, or AI.

She saw that many computer programs were built with errors. One of these programs was supposed to recognize people's faces. But it didn't work as well on people of color. If AI was going to change the world for the better, it had to be fair. The people who built these tools should look like the people who used them.

Timnit tried to fix these problems at a few different companies. But people didn't want her solutions. Or she ran into more problems. She realized if she wanted to fix AI, she'd have to start her own company.

So Timnit created a company to study how to make artificial intelligence programs better. She works every day to find a way to fix this problem, just like her family taught her.

About Rebel Girls

Rebel Girls is a global, multi-platform empowerment brand dedicated to helping raise the most inspired and confident generation of girls through content, experiences, products, and community. Originating from an international best-selling children's book, Rebel Girls amplifies stories of real-life women throughout history, geography, and field of excellence. With a growing community of nearly 20 million self-identified Rebel Girls spanning more than 100 countries, the brand engages with Generation Alpha through its book series, award-winning podcast, events, and merchandise. With the 2021 launch of the Rebel Girls app, the company has created a flagship destination for girls to explore a wondrous world filled with inspiring true stories of extraordinary women.

As a B Corp, we're part of a global community of businesses that meet high standards of social and environmental impact.

Join the Rebel Girls community:

Facebook: facebook.com/rebelgirls
Instagram: @rebelgirls
Twitter: @rebelgirlsbook
TikTok: @rebelgirlsbook
Web: rebelgirls.com
Podcast: rebelgirls.com/podcast
App: rebelgirls.com/audio

If you liked this book, please take a moment to review it wherever you prefer!